Even Christians Stumble and Fall
Musings of a Struggling Believer

by Branch Isole

Even Christians Stumble and Fall
Musings of a Struggling Believer
by Branch Isole

Library of Congress Control Number:
2004102207
ISBN 978-0974769240
eBook ISBN 978-0983574491

MANA'O PUBLISHING

Home of the VOYEURISTIC POET

Manao Publishing
Hampton, VA 23666

Order copies of this book at
www.branchisole.com
www.manaopublishing.com
www.Amazon.com
www.BarnesandNoble.com

"Many write of things known or experienced,
I comment on those seen and heard."

"I lay in Zion a stone that causes men to stumble
and a rock that makes them fall,
and the one who trusts in him
will never be put to shame."

~Romans 9:33

"If it weren't for Jesus the Christ,
I'd be a Buddhist."

Contents

Idols
John Eight Forty Seven
Kingdom of God
Letters
Longing
Lost
Miracle
Necessities
Ocular Peel
Offspring
Once Upon A Walk
Onslaught
Parenthetically
Peaceful Rest
Rapture
Relief
Repentance
Running in Place
Sinners Release
Sixty Minutes
So Easy, So Hard
Soul to Soul
Symbolic
Threefold
Third Person Singular
Twin Towers

Introduction

There are two overlapping paths in each life.
One practical, one esoteric. One material, one
spiritual. One self centered, one of service.
For searchers on every avenue of endeavor there
are times of decision as to how and what one's
response will be. This is no less true for the
Christian believer. For the repentant follower
Jesus' Spirit lives within to aid and guide along
the path.

Perhaps the greatest blessing for a Christian is
the belief of eternal life through the death and
resurrection of Jesus the Christ.

Christianity is a journey with a destination.
The Christian is blessed in that he or she has a
master teacher within whose spirit they may
abide. The examples shown to us by Jesus the
Christ teaches how to react to the events, people
and circumstances of life and are designed to
help us become more spiritually grounded and
connected.

One of the basics of Christ's teachings is lost on
many of His followers. The decision to become
a Christian and therefore to respond more
"Christ-like" is not a one-time event of
conversion. That is, we do not give our lives
over to an emulation of Jesus' thoughts, words
and deeds, and suddenly all is 'milk and honey.'

With temptations and morsels of pleasure and power to divert our new found spiritual attentions and heartfelt desires, the wiles of the world take potshots at the believer.

Learning takes place when we choose differently in problematic situations similar to those we have experienced in the past. The elapsed time between the potential options of choice and our decision of action determines the rate of our growth. Reducing to moments instead of hours, days and years the time between choice, decision and action rewards our new experience and its outcome.

God's way is not to punish, berate or belittle the stumbling believer. His essence of love and compassion are always present no matter how many times we may backslide.

God's holiness requires that He admonish errant choices and aberrant behavior in order to encourage learning and growth in the life of the believer.

Christians stumble and fall as testaments to their faith of God's invited grace in their lives. We must "take up our cross daily" because *we are going to stumble and fall* while on our path.

This book is about moments of decision when once more we are righted and are about to take that next step after being pulled, pushed or voluntarily leaving the believers walk.

May these musings help strengthen your resolve to walk a little further down the path of spiritual enlightenment, learning and growth.

Branch Isole

"Morality may perhaps consist solely in the courage of making a choice."

~Leon Blum (1872-1950)
French Statesman

Abandoned Never

Lord open my mind
that I might know Your Word
Open my heart
that I might learn Your Ways
Open my eyes
that I might see Your Truth
This,
and every new day

Fill me with Your love
Your simple Commands
That I might now better understand

Not forgetting my past
my sins
my transgressions,
but living anew
with forgiving intentions

You have always been here
Now, that's perfectly clear
It is I who was blind
refusing to see
Spent the time thinking
it was all about me

Fill the void
which lives within me
Mend the break
within my heart
Become one with my conscience again
From this moment, We start

Absence

Days grow shorter
The end times approach
Our struggles increase
Your children look
to you for relief,
Still you do not answer

We've known four hundred years of silence
twice experienced without you
your back turned in disgust
Our convenient lifestyles
daily tests for us

Crying out for release
for guidance,
answers
You respond as you please;
as rock
solid stone
only your back exposed
from upon your throne

Is it the false prophets
we choose to follow
or the carnality
in which we wallow
Keeping hidden from our view
muffling our ears
silencing you

You gaze into our hearts
filled with science and art
A burgeoning, blistering world
the home of lust and greed
its festering pustules bleed
spreading covetous cankers
as ripened roots of disease

We shout out your name
then spit upon it, taking it in vain
when you fail to acknowledge us
immediately

Avoidance

God, How Great Thou Art
that you would use your awesome powers
to allow each of us to live on
and be in your presence eternally
merely by believing in you
and recognizing your spirit
in the one you sent;
Our way of reconciliation
Our redeemer thwarting death
Our councilor of wisdom
A mediator for our sinfulness

Awareness of our spirit within
living forever
is beyond our imagination
It is an understanding impossible for us to grasp
in its sublime enormity

We who live from moment to moment
day by day
counting the years
as if they were capsules of permanence
in which to invest

Overlooking your purpose for each;
To come closer to the blessings you offer
for obedience and belief
You ask nothing more of us
and yet,
we spend life's time and energy
finding all manner of excuse
to avoid you and your word

Bad

guilt is fear of retribution
not absence of reward
exhibited by shame
when sensing one's own lack
of ethical and moral character

the overwhelming emotion of unworthiness
exists between you and your beliefs,
not you and God

His self sacrifice
has freed you of complicity with sin

Baseline

There are no more degrees of hypocrisy,
than there are of sin

Believing is Seeing

God's desire;
that His sovereign majesty as creator
be recognized and acknowledged

God's wish;
to be joined by all
who recognize a place in his family
and acknowledge the brotherhood of man

God's hope;
that each will recognize His spirit
in the one He sent
and acknowledge His son's
redemptive and reconciliatory purpose

God's demand;
that each of us make our own decision
as to whether we will recognize
and acknowledge
Him, His Spirit and His Son

Choices

The game or the gift
The lust or the love
The darkness or light
The loss, or blessing from above.

You approach with your thoughts.

War and peace
Aloneness and pleasing
Poverty and pleasure
Listening to them and hearing you,

You allow us to know our deeds.

Poetry, prose
Parable lessons
The words flow in statements
from each learning session.

You teach us by your word.

Your guarantee; our release.

Clarity

Strip away the veneer
Dry insecurity's tear
Remove all blinders
Put down your mask
Rend the veils of illusion

See, to embrace truth

Come and Get It

Hey There
modern Christian couple
accumulating more accoutrements
to help you through the months ahead?
A second story home addition
swimming pool and third new truck
for you it's obviously
more than luck

The Lord must be blessing you
with those expensive things
We even stole a peek
at your new four carat ring

The seasons have changed
as again they should
Interesting how it all unfolds
along the lines He said it would

Where does fleeting time get to?
We wonder and wish
we had a clue
We notice you've made
a few improvements,
maybe one or two?

Marble floors of Italian Terrazzo
A double oven-stove-microwave
cooking combo
and oh, your latest designer wardrobe too
Perhaps we should start
attending church with you

Reluctantly it appears
we're living in the dark
Don't get us wrong
we love the Lord
but for us it's simply
in our hearts

We'll hang in there
and try to get by
vicariously living your joy
With the advent of each shiny new purchase
and every additional toy

By the way
we thought we'd ask
if it happens
to come to pass,
our faith falls short
proving not enough
and the Rapture comes
taking you and leaving us
As surviving sinners
we would be,
May we have all your stuff?

Conundrum

Superior Mothers
The meek and the faint
Offender, and faithful saint
He who borrowed, he who lent
She who was broken
They whom were bent
The graft soaked politician
The murderous Mafia Don
The conniving thieving securities broker
The lying cheating heinous stalker
The serial killer along for the ride
The dictator promulgating genocide
Each and every free will sins
Together in line
all wait to be forgiven

Cry Uncle

God I'm so over you
strung along from pillar to post
elevated pinnacle highs
with summit swirls of illusion
perpetrated to bring me down
cowering in submission
to prove what point,
your superiority?

You, all powerful in this relationship
yet the strength of your authority
depends upon my submissive acquiescence,
otherwise, what have you actually gained?

Your humble presentation
masks a wrath of purpose
Except that it is your perpetuation, not mine
Should I fade into oblivion who is disappointed
You or me?
You I fear.
For you shall go on
recognizing and understanding loss
while I will have become
but a distant memory
passed to nothingness, to all except you

then will you cry for me?
Unconditionally?

Death Rests

If the choice between death
and eternal life rests
ultimately on the words
of Jesus the Christ
whereby he asks each
to believe in their heart
and express with their voice
a new spiritual place
from which to start;
that he came here
the Word to spread
that he was in fact
whom he said

God wants for nothing
and needs nothing more
than each to respond
to His knock at their door

No good deeds nor merits
riches or fame
merely believe
and attest to His name

Believe He came down
from heaven on high
to save us little gods
from Satanic lies

A sublime expression
of understood belief
who is creator
and whom causes self grief

Why not today?
tomorrow for sure!

Accept Jesus' role, as he did

His sacrifice for sinners
which turns each new believer
into eternity's winner

What have you to lose?
except life everlasting
for stepping down from your pedestal
and throwing open your senses
to reach across infinity's fences

How great His love:
a desire for you with Him forever?
He'll wait until your last breath
when one foot inside death's door are you led
to finally believe
what Jesus the Christ
hath said

Dreams and Schemes

Dreaming
Scheming
Trying to make it so
But what is *It*?

A moment?
This week?
The next phase?
Living by the newest idiom
or latest craze?

Parroting today's tonal
"15 Minutes" phrase?
Becoming part of the current fad or trend?
Which way today blow the winds of change?
To where and what now
does our willpower bend?

Hurrying life
Growing up fast
Experiences anew
No growth from the past
Same mistakes made
Despondencies tumble
causing foundations to crumble
producing emotional gravel
as another mosaic relationship unravels

Ignoring lessons
designed to be learned
Omitting ones
which should have become ingrained
forgotten tears, disregarded pain

New money making ideas
put past failures to rest
New possession goals;
better
bigger
best

The same me
The same you
Growing older
Different view
Day by day
each relying
upon the other
for reassurance
all is okay

But is it?
Will it be?
Hiding behind
wanton dreams
Running to
controlling schemes

Proceeding without caution
racing into the trap
set by life
Filled with further
lies and deceits
until our day
of mortal sleep

And all the while
in our hearts we knew
Our quest would have indeed been blessed
if our search had been,
for you

For in the end
what is this world
and all its temptations,
except a lamenting backward look
at unfulfilled dreams
and well worn schemes

Emotional Expenditures

The cost to the heart
Can be all or nothing,
But the currency of love
Is commitment

End of Days

Each day she looks forward to the next
In singularity she anticipates its end
for each end brings rest
and a separate peace

It is there,
in quiet moments
hollowed out
from the world's daily noise
that her closed eye visions
blossom into glory's landscape,
stretching endlessly
in all directions

A brief respite
from the malaise of age
and its chronological erosion of matter
gives sense to mind and spirit
of the unbounded serenity, which awaits
just beyond
the end of days

Exchanges

Changes
these past years
so slight, so subtle
almost imperceptibly
have we changed.

Growth of character
has taken over
as age continues to ravage
the physical lust we once knew,
the cravings which were once us
in the beginning.

We look deeper now.
See more.
Understand easier.

We've become more complete
More inseparable
More as one,
There is no me, no you
There is only us.

Oral assignation
no longer needed
as we finish each other's sentences
in words, in thoughts.

Our bodies meld
as if some morphed entity
of science fiction.

Telepathically
our spirits touch
and explore each other
as exchanges in energies, ideas and being
glide through the universe
and return home body bound
to roost and rest.

Preparations for enlightened freedom
to be shared together
before the throne seat of God
One together, one with all
One with truth and love,
eternally.

An extinguished flame
Light traded for dark
In that moment
One last shared thought,
soul mates.

For The

For the drunk
it's his barstool
at his favorite place

For the super model
it's 'the look'
upon the face

For the sports fan
it's Sunday afternoon

For the musician
it's all
in the tune

For the depressed
it's in the confines
of a room

For the sycophant
it's in the glory
or the doom

For each and every one
it's different
Whether explore, expose
explode or exploit
Each has their own way
to fill the void

The emptiness of heart
A sense of despair
Avoiding the mirror's eyes
The ones that stare

For those in the mirror
know the truth,
and the truth is always
one hundred proof

When truth fills the void
as a hand in a glove
then in tandem lives
compassion and love

A heart with these three
is always triumphant
no matter the case
or what it may be

How does one acquire
said precious jewels?
Of the book, inquire
and use daily
it's tools

Start prior to death,
as close as possible to birth
The title of this Holy Grail?
Basic Instructions Before Leaving Earth.

Forever

Only the finite mind grapples
with the shear conceptual enormity
of
Forever

Only Spirit
void of decay
can endure the non-physical being
of
Forever

Only God has experienced
the a priori existence
of
Forever

Yet through his abiding concern and love
He offers to the Christian believer of His Word
Revelation of one's a posteriori existence
of
Forever

Forgiveness

Forget it,
I have.

Four Score

Designing, developing, discovering
the first twenty spent
with family, school, peers
influential environment
foundation's formative years
of who, what we become
shiftless aristocrat, magnificent bum
Fleshing out
puffing up
identifying
the straw men erected
for our conjured lying

Second score purportments; 'it's all about me'
shackled by economic chains
mumbled claims of being free

Surviving incongruence
within shells, behind masks
Layers of self doubt, rampant insecurities
behind facades used to bask

Forty to sixty, the toughest of all
opportunities to shine, vexing chances to fall

What to believe
if we still be here
Knowledge, understanding
of quadrant four
Existential plumb line measuring
our seasoned role

Coming to terms
Contributions?
Reconciling the pleasure
the pain,
the glory
the shame
Finale;
resting peace
one more try
New being, New name

Fundamentalists

The true believer wants to prove
he is not afraid to die,
yet is he ready to die
as a testament to his faith

the Atheist wants to prove
all belief a lie
the Muslim wants to prove
he is right
the Buddhist wants to prove
he is on the path
the Hindu wants to prove
he can best himself
the Jew wants to prove
no pharisaic mistake
the Christian wants to prove
the Word he was given is true

God desires to prove,
He is faithful to all

God's Fault

It's compelling to observe
the Christian
stumble and fall,
straying from God's
prescriptive path of obedience,
as the prince of darkness
cogently wiles and wills the self righteous
with indulgent temptations

Not credited to the devil
the Christian's acquiesced falter
upon hitting rock bottom
or being mired in the swill
Newly crowned
these worldly winners
bemoan the gestures of a God
who has turned his back
in refusal to placate their sins

Hamlet Wondered

"To Be or Not To Be"

Who do you expect to see
after you have passed away?
Family, friends
your dog, your cat
Jesus Christ
T.S. Geisel of "The Cat in the Hat?"

Have you made your plans
for that first breath,
the first one, after your last?

Your future
becomes your present
but what about your past?

Will you be prepared
with a readied point of reference?
Do you need a compass rose
and will you know the difference?

Will you be seeing
a light
in the dark
at a tunnel's end?

Are you anticipating multitudes
to join you before a throne

Or a single
final
anxious moment,
all alone?

Have you been covered
by your beliefs
against all negativity?
Is it necessary,
for you
for them
for your worst enemy,
your best friend?

Once all is said and done
After this world's victory is won
and you are just a memory
where will you be?

Does it even matter?
Salient and silent thoughts please. . .

"To Be or Not To Be"

Heartfelt

Fulfillment of the heart
with the coveted things
of this world
is reflected in such as;
size, color and cost
Blinding us to Him
who truly fulfills,
and may be eternally lost

Horizon

An original thought?
A conundrum
A quandary
All lest one proven scientifically

Franklin's kite and key,
electricity
Sir Isaac's falling apple,
gravity
Einstein's time and space,
relativity
Along with all the others
each and every one, shown empirically

but a Triune Godhead's eternal existence
too much, to be believed?
No method to define mathematically
A proof of three in one, one in three,
Each must simply die, for to see

I Don't Need You God

I Don't Need You God
To guide my way
through the night
or the day
Upon this path
is your loving light
which I will follow
unto the last

I Don't Need You God
to talk to me
about your word
Believe me Lord
our quests are in reach
I'll learn, You Teach

I Don't Need You God
to be near
awaiting to be asked
You always dry every tear
when it's in your love we bask

I Don't Need You God
to take my hand
in order to better
understand
Your Word is the wisdom
which quenches life's thirst
extinguishes the fires
of ignorance

I Don't Need You God
I can do it all
on my own
As long as you walk with me
from here
to your throne

I Don't Need You God
except I do,
and each time I ask
petition or pray
you surround me
with you, night and day

My life is not
as we wanted it to be
but you've stayed the course
and from the beginning
it was I who wavered
stumbled and fell
While you remained steadfast
my doubts to quell

Although you're always here
I know your blessing
for me oh Lord
is that you won't interfere

Idols

The idols to which we bow and pay homage
spit on us and our insecurities.
They are created by us
that we might recognize something greater
than we
And the farthest we gaze
is to ourselves as their creators.

It may be one thing to create,
quite another to bestow blessings.
Playing at God does not equate to being God
any more than the ego to create,
bears blessings.

What greater self-duplicity
than to be the creators of our own idols
to which we then bow down?

Our identity crisis
cries out
for understanding and recognition.
Cries out
to all and any who would listen
with deaf ears,
as if to hear.

We cry and wonder
"How can I be so full of void?"
With passion we trade our blood, sweat and tears
for the things of this world
While giving little. . . or worse,
"lukewarm" commitment
to the essence of life -
a personal spiritual relationship with God.

For the Spiritual Christian
everything needed, all facets in place
It is the choice of our heart
that determines our mask,
our cover,
our face.

Our actions; the seeds,
each new day do we sow
We always get
what we really want
That is for each
of us to know

Be it cash
or sacred cow
The questions are
to where, and to whom
will we bow?

John Eight Forty Seven

You have but requested
we recognize your name
yet modern day apostles
coerce through guilt's shame
Unable to accept balance
on the path of peace
their goal separation
keeping you and we at extremes

Their declarations of you;
Wrath
Compassion
Unattainable, Forgiveness
Yet it is we who give them power
to decide our fate
it is we who allow their extortion
of our emotional state

Never your way
The truth be told
Only one intermediary between you and us
One teacher, advocate, lord
He, who went to the cross

This glut of self-righteous
false prophets unnecessary
in order to belong to you,
for you have explained simple and true
our instructions from heaven
understand the relationship pronounced
in John 8:47

Kingdom of God

Love's eternal presence
On earth, as it is in heaven
is shown
is known
As His sun again rises
each new day, one of seven

The Kingdom of God
Now and forever
Revealed to us
To each who would see
His kingdom
His presence
Always will be

Through His spirit
Flesh made real
That all might hear
His final appeal

Come to Me
Through my Word,
My Son
That you might know how
your race against death
will finally be won,
For your soul to live
not once, but twice
Your salvation
Your redemption
is found in the Christ

Letters

Dear God,

You put us in
this selfish place
Controlling species
our human race

Full of Temptations
Choices
Deadly sins
We love filling
our hearts
with them

Refusing responsibility
for outcomes different
than pre-conceived

Fighting for celebrity
today one's name
is the game

Oh hallelujah
to be like you God
where everyone knows
who you are,
number one
most famous
the biggest
the best,
known by all
more than all the rest

You can't hold me responsible
for all the mistakes I've made
You're to blame
for me being as I am
by the way

You gave me choices
and freedoms to decide
which outlandish
lame excuse to use
as my next lie,
I'm here struggling
trying to get by

P.S. Yes I know
It's been a while,
since I've thought of you
Longer still
since we last talked
A lifetime if the truth be told
from when our spirits
were interlocked

P.P.S. And Lord
just one more little thing
Now that you know
I'm still here
Send more money
if it pleases you,
a Vegas jackpot or lottery will do

Longing

Vacillating
between calm and seismic agitation
her cognition of self
revisits today's reality
Once again, realization;
the pangs of pain
coming and going
are unique to her
and this morphing physique
within which she is imprisoned

Soreness, redness
Tumultuous bodily functions
Toes, tendons, teeth
from cranial to podiatric
Psychosomatic or real?
she prays, awaiting relief

Skimming with surface friction
static agitation beneath

A vibrant mind, trapped
in limbo, hovers
as a bucket, dangled
amid a deep dark well

Sensing a progressive wearing away
from years of unattended use
built upon specific indulgent abuse
gives way now
to millions of conjoined
and layered aging cells

Maleficent, misfiring neurons
exhibit evidence where no injurious state exists
Longing for stasis
Caught precariously between
the will to die and a desire to live
she now understands the reward for belief
and escape unto the gateway of eternity

Lost

The world labeled me wild,
But you knew me lost
Sin invited me in,
Only you knew the cost

Season by season
I stumbled and fell,
Only you knew
I was headed for hell

Unable to scrape together
The dollars for bail,
The old judge just smiled
And sent me to jail
The next time we met
There were no tears,
The old judge just smiled
and said, "99 years."

I sit in my cell
And stare at the sink
All alone now
With more time to think

No friends to joke with
Party or drink
I sit in my cell
And stare at the sink

Alone and forgotten
Rotting away
Chalk on the wall
One slash for each day

What would I give
To do it again
What would I give
To be in your pen

To be one of your sheep
Instead of a goat
To hear your voice
My final hope
To hear your voice
To know your word
To follow your will
Finally, free as a bird

A free bird still caged
Age after age
Trimmed and clipped wings
No longer enraged

Day after day
One step closer to death
No longer caged
Now, finally at rest
No longer alone
Having passed through your cross
Now flying with you Lord,
No longer lost.

Miracle

The miracle of life is this;
against all odds save one
in a redacted moment
betwixt frolic and fun,
did the sparks of energy and matter combine
producing your chance to eternally exist

Necessities

It becomes necessary to focus
on the things of the world
because the relief offered by God
for turning from things of the world
presents itself as a reward
only in response
to our inability to gain the things of the world
upon which we focus

Our obsession with worldly ways
might be put aside
if we were fulfilled by the way of peace
which God keeps obsessively hidden

We strive to conquer and provide
that we might honor God
through the oblations of our victories,
yet unless we give up
our crowns and surrender
He snubs our offerings

He put us here that we might reconnect
with Him through reliance,
and when we relent
He withdraws farther
to further test our resilience

Without hope and perseverance
our struggles would be scored
by wins and losses,
but then we would be oblivious
to the guilt and shame
which feeling unworthy produces,
and our lives would be ours again

Ocular Peel

your disciples love to proselytize
your Omnipotent control
according to a plan,
that all are accepted
by Omnivision forgiving eyes

if stone hearted pharaohs be necessity
to empower each Moses' stuttered words
because your children
turn away, refuse
through ebbing flows of their own
why not enlighten the Devil's given,
their earned dues

even You
can't have it
both ways

covenant Apostle claimants
your Word true told
suffering your promise
against a world's indifference
caring not one way or the other
the struggles cuckold
within your fold

sending One to save the sinners;
condemning free will
you chose to give,
your stymied efforts
against a preponderance of proof
does Jobian faith, yet still live?

prescriptive control;
disruptive choice or election
to remain under a thumb,
damning disdain
you abjectly object
to relinquish your own

at odds;
the guilt of conscience
you supplied
against the tests
for your forgiving eyes

Offspring

Truth
is the proving ground
for Love
in our search of worthiness

to stave off indifference
and disappointment
of our recognition
for approval

Once Upon A Walk

Stick
and Bone
and Leaf
and Rock
these four I found
while on my walk

Stick once lived and now is dead
Bone having come from some skeletal head
Leaf has turned from green to reddish gold
all part of the process of growing old

and Rock, what of you
from whence have you come
from what part
of the original load
were you taken
to be part of this road

you, small Rock with your family and friends
all joined together here, here at the end
end of the lane, end of the street
without you mighty Rock
no route is complete

it is you mighty Rock who forms
the foundation,
the path and the way,
for a wandering nation

mighty Rock, it is upon your back
that Stick
and Bone
and Leaf
do alight
during the day
and during the night

each at the end of their personal race
looking to you for a loving embrace
for it is only upon you mighty Rock
from your passionate grace,
that Stick
and Bone
and Leaf
find their final resting place.

Onslaught

In our search for something greater
than ourselves
we overlook the simplicity of God;
love
truth
forgiveness

Caught up in minutia of our own making
we misinterpret the purpose of His plan

Fading into the distance
Camouflaged by shadows
of here and now 'necessities'
we wallow in worldly ways

Our temporal desires quickened
by short sighted goals,
a collective
quest for lust,
disbelief in truth,
failure to forego insecurities
serve to bolster blindness
of our inadequacies

For we have a plan and purpose
far greater than His of future
yet the thieves of life;
approval
status
recognition

thrust us competitively
against the wall of legacy
accounting for the length of imprint
we might make,
as if it mattered
beyond the pages of history

Steeped in rebellion
by our nature
we are encouraged to drift
farther and farther away,
and we delight in the passage

it is not He
who has turned His back,
it is we

Parenthetically

The cruelty of life
is that we only live once
(the blessing,
we only die once)

Peaceful Rest

There's no way
we can save ourselves
there's nothing we can do
No matter how righteous
we may become
our sinful nature
still resides within
Osmotically saturating thoroughly
through and through

Then why not give up
Throw in the towel
Why not
have it our way
Why not
bask in sin's pleasurable angst
Each night, Every day

If God's promise
is to save us
from our sinful selves
why struggle to know His Word
With His single statement
of reconciled resurrection,
is not that the totality
of what we need to learn?

He's prepared to give,
because He already gave
freeing each from bondage
of being sin's willing slave
Why not live a scoundrel's life
and come round with our last breath?
The revelation is. . .
We can!
and in Him peacefully rest

To God
each sin committed
is equal to any other
No more, no less,
a sin is a sin
The point is finally
to come to Him

Recite and truly repent
changing in His sight
Ask His forgiveness
Be prepared to see
His compassionate
loving
forgiving light

Rapture

A hard and difficult life
to this place were you led
Troubled souls, tumultuous times
survival mode
constant dread
Culmination of all earthly fears
tested,
in three short years

Exposed to the best
and the worst of us
You, unconditional love
with never a fuss

Offered everything there is
was,
or ever might be
Offered all both man
and the Devil could find
And all you wanted
were the sins and burdens
of all mankind

You could only come once
to set the stage
A triumphant return
in the next age

When shall that be?
Some wait and wonder
when believer and non
will be put asunder
Your words ring true now
as they did then

"In my story
all is shown
Signs, wonders, miracles
by these
they should have known
For those of you here
some intent
some sublime
one day all
will see the sign"

"When this age is over,
and finally done
and into the next
you each finally come
Out of Pisces
and into Aquarius
for it is then
all life shall end
Except for those
whom I call friend"

"My words are clear
for each of you here
Now is the time
to be made aware
of the fortieth day
marked after the event
that fulfilled the role
for which I was sent"

"I mentioned often
for all who have ears
Trust and follow me,
You'll have nothing to fear"

"Heed if you will
all sheep and all goats
My task assigned
to judge every folk
To judge all the same
and deliver into His name,
those who chose to believe
and lived obediently"

"Before the last day's time
there are decisions to be made
by reason and rhyme
Not only for yourself
but for those whom you love
that none might be lost
but ascend to above"

"It is your choice,
It is up to you,
To know where you'll be
when this age is through"

"Will you now choose
to believe,
and prepare your family
for what lies ahead?

Or ignore God's Word
and continue to be part
of the world's walking dead?"

Relief

How many untold billions have come and gone
While the finger of God
has touched His handful
that they might propel mankind
farther along His designed path
of reconciliation

progressively built upon
an expanding man's legacy
at each turn and fork in the road
the battle, the struggle, the conflict
of choice
might be easier understood
yet harder to make

within each field of endeavor
He has guided
by His will
those, His instruments of change
in art and industry
that they would give hope and expectation
to a stunned and shocked mass of humanity
waiting for . . .
anticipating . . .
relief

Repentance

"Am I to stand trial?"
tentatively she asked
with doe eyed innocence
so long ago practiced
and perfected
Her feigned look
at the ready,
the one she uses if ever
she's rejected

"Trial" he responded
"Oh no,
Nothing quite so dramatic
Nothing quite so traumatic"

"Your soul atonement
to be made today
is only for those sins
made along the way
Temptations you gave into
Those you traversed
while waiting for this day
on mother earth"

"Those committed
after repentance
Those which tempted
causing you to slip
Those you gave into
after begging forgiveness
with parted lips"

For all women and men
The difference between
eternal light and dark
is related to the place
God occupies
in the heart

Running in Place

Fear of retribution
Angst of restitution
of and for the one unknown
Faithless acts of sin
conflicts born within
all set in motion at origin
Refusal to listen, to heed
feud between spirit and flesh
at stake, eternal rest

Standing in line, pleading
for the opportunity once more to chance
an earth bound experience, lifetime
Redemption to resurrect

unable to provide relief
forgiveness on the tip of the tongue
unwilling to unleash words of surrender
keep us bound by this one

As time runs out
in both heaven and earth
Held in the balance
our release from cyclical pain
disguised as freedom won

Sinners Release

Reaching a breaking point,
full of anger
frustration
disdain
For all there is
or might be ahead
each day holds the same refrain

Why is it Lord
even in our surrender
you insist on being so hard?
Is the guilt of our sins
not enough for your name?
Do you smile as we wallow
in our shame?

Giving up on life is easy
once realization sets in
no matter the brief moments
of reduced lamenting
one comes to know finally
there's no way to win

Pulled back and forth
eventually down,
into the dust to be trampled
Surrender doesn't seem
to be quite enough
It's difficult to imagine you
sporting a grin

Explain if you would
when we've reached for too much,
the holy version
of your tough love

You desire us to be thankful,
and we are,
for your guiding and honest words
Were we perfect
we would not need be here
Striving constantly
you've made it clear,
that's not enough

Now we're torn as to what to do,
go back?
turn on you?
Rely again on selves of old?
Once and for all embrace the ways of the world?
Allow the dawn of chaos to unfold?

For you are God
and we are not
From you we expect more
than we do from ourselves
Perhaps that's why so many return
to rebellion's open door

No longer caring
it's the tic in the spasm
of falling again,
which frustrates you and we
yet at least there,
in disobedience
lies sin's sense of being free

Sixty Minutes

One hour to go
if it would only
go slow,
waiting,
while knowing
there is no control,
no relief
waiting now
upon the thief

Thief in the night
thief of life
nemesis of the living
always taking,
never giving

Last breath
Last thought
Last vision
Last words,
what will they be?

The final realization
a plea for reconstitution
an act of reinstatement
perhaps reincarnation,
A cry for forgiveness

To look eye to eye
with the one,
the Christ,
or
to face the heat
to sleep and wait,
which
is the slated fate

Minutes left
only a few
the choice,
eternity
to win or lose.

So Easy, So Hard

those who don't understand Christianity
those who condemn Christianity
those who resist Christianity
are misinterpreting *the definitive* example of
unconditional love

God could have made His right of passage
a difficult test or chore
He could have insisted on some long,
treacherous journey
to some far off foreign shore
filled with threatening obstacles
and harrowing experiences
He could have required sacrifice
or proof of accomplishment
from each Pilgrim serious

but He didn't

In lieu of strife
He asks *only*
one's acknowledged confession;
He himself made the journey
and paid redemption's price

"God. . . i believe"
His sole requirement
for everlasting life

Of all who would pass
through this world reviled
He himself came to reconcile
for only His power and providence
could trump His own sentence of death
for disobedience

Could acceptance of His invitation
for an eternal existence be easier?
and yet,
those who refuse to believe
choose not to believe
for they have their reasons

Preferring to toil in the tasks
and dwell in the gaiety of rebellion
to His loving consideration

They cannot bring themselves
to utter
those three words

Soul to Soul

We look beyond the bounds of flesh
to the aura of being
We stare beneath the here and now
to see revealed the connection between we three

Having matured and shared the vulnerabilities of
growth's path
we gaze hypnotically
realizing none of the world's
temporary pleasures
is enough to separate these two souls
from devotion

Exposed in marriage vows of the newly wed
Heard but not, veiled by approved opportunity
of lust's long awaited desires
the years far off in future's distance
our adventure begins,
not soul filled
but organic and prodigious by design

There will be time enough to discover the one
with whom we must learn to live with and about

There will be time enough to discover
the oblation which waits
in the shadows of unconditional love

Allowing us freedom to explore
the esotericism of the abstract
through the base of being,
we come closer to eternity
with each step of understanding
and acceptance of each other

Our love grows, transcending from
"milk to meat"
that our souls may harmoniously join the choir
and chorus of heaven
in praise
to the completeness of the cosmos

Symbolic

It was necessary for Jesus of Nazareth
to live and die in an era
when the executioner's tool was the cross

For no other symbol of demeaning elevation
could have evolved to have such impact

Threefold

There exists a threefold purpose
in Christian scripture
for the heart
and mind
and soul of the believer

Realization there is
an unconditional parental love
who at all times has
our best interests at heart.

Personal knowledge of an advocate
who laid down his life
on our behalf
and in our stead.

A spiritual understanding
we are not alone
as we face adversities.

Third Person Singular

A friend of mine was taken ill today
one day he'll be taken even farther away
Caught between each, body and mind
exists the One who has lived for all time

The essence of being
who lived with the Light
traveled the darkness
pierced the night

Finding anew a new spot to dwell
a transient place betwixt heaven and hell
Third Person of this spiritual existence
joins together mind and body
without initial resistance
A new life of joy
trials, tribulations and tests
Decisions and choices before final rest
Along the treacherous path
good times and bad,
compassion and wrath

Genderless being of eternal spirit
Third Person watcheth and intently heareth
the conversation
which mind has to say
as body slips further into decay

"Give me rest,
I've done my best"
cries out body's punished flesh
"I'm nowhere near ready
to leave this place
I've just now started
to understand its pace"
retorts now knowing mind
"Realizing the cost
of gain against loss
I'm in need
of a little more time"

Conflict persists
Third Person waits
Aware examination,
exemption
both wait at the gate

Assigned a task
of eternal immunity
Disguised by a mask
of temporary impunity

Mind and Body
drift further apart
Less and less stress,
Now a flat lining chart
Once more
Third Person free,
to stand again
before the Trinity

Mind knew of life
and so too with Body
Third Person's role
the duty of soul,
to bring together
once and for all
three standing anew
never again to fall

Twin Towers

We come into the world
knowing
We are not aware however
that we know
Hence, our struggle begins

Consciousness from His breath
Conscience from His fingertip touch
Knowledge, our sole connection to God
is carried over
and brought forth with us,
from the light
into the darkness
Hence, our struggle begins

It is here, in this time and place
the kernel,
that seedling of ethic
is watered by
guilt
shame
embarrassment
Hence, our struggle begins

Conflicts rage past
as do the years
played out within our
choices, decisions, responses
to people and events that shape
the Twin Towers of our struggle,
Right and Wrong

Storyteller Branch Isole is the author of nineteen books. Born in Osaka Japan, Branch traveled extensively growing up calling many places home. Finishing high school in Southern California, he went on to graduate from Texas State University, attended graduate school at the University of Houston and received an M.A. Theology degree from Trinity Bible College and Seminary.

His catalogue of work includes books, eBooks, greeting cards and inspirational gift mats, available at

www.branchisole.com
www.manaopublishing.com

Other books by Branch Isole
Poetic Prose Series

Heartstrings of Illusion ©
Distractions and Deceit in Poetic Prose
ISBN 978-0982658543
eBook ISBN 978-0983574545

Dreams and Schemes ©
Tales and Tattles in Poetic Prose
ISBN 978-0982658550
eBook ISBN 978-0983574552

In The Margins ©
where truth lies
ISBN 978-0982658536
eBook ISBN 978-0983574538

Eclectic Electricity ©
unknown poet's parade
ISBN 978-0982658512
eBook ISBN 978-0983574521

Turn Of A Phrase ©
Pivotal Positions in Poetic Prose
ISBN 978-0982658505
eBook ISBN 978-0983574514

Saccharin and Plastic Band Aids ©
Comments in Poetic Prose
ISBN 978-0974769288
eBook ISBN 978-0983574453

Messages In A Bottle ©
Inspirations in Poetic Prose
ISBN 978-0974769295
eBook ISBN 978-0983574446

Reflections On Chrome ©
Parking Lot Confessions in Poetic Prose
ISBN 978-0974769257
eBook ISBN 978-0983574422

Postcards from the Line of Demarcation ©
Points of Separation in Poetic Prose
ISBN 978-0974769264
eBook ISBN 978-0983574439

Seeds of Mana'o ©
Thoughts, Ideas and Opinions in Poetic Prose
ISBN 978-0974769219
eBook ISBN 978-0983574415

Barking Geckos ©
Stories and Observations in Poetic Prose
ISBN 978-0974769226
eBook ISBN 978-0983574408

Anthologies

Crucibles ©
Refinement of the Neophyte Christian
ISBN 978-0974769233
eBook ISBN 978-0983574484

Power of Praise ©
Poetry of Spiritual Christianity ™
ISBN 978-0974769271
eBook ISBN 978-0983574477

Epigram ©
long story short
ISBN 978-0982658574
eBook ISBN 978-0983574576

Orgy of Words ©
Salacious Short Stories in Poetic Prose
ISBN 978-0982658529
eBook ISBN 978-0983574569

Self Improvement

GOD. . .i believe ©
Simple Steps on the Path
of Spiritual Christianity ™
ISBN 978-0974769202
eBook ISBN 978-0983574460

Pathways to Publishing ©
Self Publishing
Manuscript to Publication
ISBN 978-0982658567
eBook ISBN 978-0983574507

Seduction ©
Pleasing Women Sexually
ISBN 978-0982658598
eBook ISBN 978-0983574583

www.ingramcontent.com/pod-product-compliance
Lightning Source LLC
LaVergne TN
LVHW011358080426

835511LV00005B/333